Israel's War on Gaza

Israel's War on Gaza

Gilbert Achcar

Resistance Books

Israel's War on Gaza

Gilbert Achcar

Cover design by Adam Di Chiara

Published December 2023
Resistance Books, London
info@resistancebooks.org
www.resistancebooks.org

ISBN: 978-1-872242-19-4 (print)
ISBN: 978-1-872242-20-0 (e-book)

CONTENTS

CONTENTS

Gilbert Achcar is a Lebanese socialist and Professor of Development Studies and International Relations at SOAS, University of London. His many books include: *The Clash of Barbarisms: The Making of the New World Disorder*; *Perilous Power: The Middle East and U.S. Foreign Policy*, with Noam Chomsky; *The Arabs and the Holocaust: The Arab-Israeli War of Narratives*; *The People Want: A Radical Exploration of the Arab Uprising*; and *The New Cold War: The United States, Russia and China, from Kosovo to Ukraine*.

Foreword

Operation Al-Aqsa's Flood launched by the Islamic Resistance Movement (Hamas) on 7 October 2023 was seized by Israel to launch its most murderous onslaught ever on the Palestinian people in Gaza, a narrow territory of 365 km² (141 square miles) with a population of 2.4 million inhabitants, and therefore one of the highest population densities on earth with close to 6,510 persons by km² (16,855 per square mile) including a high proportion of children. In the first six weeks of this massacre of genocidal proportions, 14,000 persons were killed, including 5,600 children (40%).

This book includes five articles about the ongoing events: the first one was written on 8 October, the day after Al-Aqsa's Flood; the second on the 16 October. Both were initially published on my blog (available on my website gilbert-achcar.net), reproduced on various websites in English, and translated into several languages. The third piece was published on 23 October in *New Lines* magazine: it was also posted by various websites and translated into several languages. The fourth and fifth pieces are translated from my weekly column in Arabic in *Al-Quds al-Arabi*, a daily newspaper based in London: they were published there on 31 October and 28 November.

The sixth and final piece provides some background to the ongoing massacre: it is an interview that Daniel Finn did with me for the *Irish Left* Review in 2009. In this interview, I explained the following, which is highly relevant to the present war:

> The 33-Day War in 2006 was already the most brutal aggression in the long history of Israeli wars, the most brutal utilization of power by Israel, carpet-bombing whole regions of Lebanon, civilian areas. The pretext then as now is that fighters are hiding among the population. This is the most hypocritical argument: what do they want them to do, to regroup in some wasteland with

signposts saying 'Bomb us here'? This is pre-posterous. The truth is that Israel is trying to crush mass political parties, which are armed, of course, but they have to be armed because they are permanently under threat. These are armed popular movements. Most of their armed members are not professional fighters living in barracks. When you take all these aspects of the problem into consideration, there are very, very serious grounds for the mounting, increasing worries that are expressed by international humanitarian agencies.

A lot of people now sense that the population of Gaza is really under threat of massive extermination. This is not the usual kind of exaggeration, it is a sober assessment when you face such a level of violence and brutality, day after day, with more and more so-called accidents in which concentrations of civilians are targeted with mass-murder as a result. The only alternative to a fiasco for Israel is to push forward its ground offensive in the populated areas. The worst-case scenario becomes therefore quite possible, and that would mean thousands and thousands of people killed, not to mention the maimed and wounded, and that is absolutely frightening.

This is indeed a very accurate description of what is occurring now under our eyes, with the open support of Western governments still refusing at the time of writing to call for a ceasefire, that is, a cessation of the massacre, thus making themselves accomplices of this massacre of genocidal proportions combined with a blatant instance of 'ethnic cleansing' – both being crimes against humanity in international law.

Gilbert Achcar, 30 November 2023

1

Initial comments on Hamas's October counter-offensive

The counter-offensive launched by Hamas against Israel on 7 October 2023, a day after the 50th anniversary of another Arab surprise attack on Israel — the October 1973 War, is a much more spectacular feat than the latter. Whereas fifty years ago, the two Arab states of Egypt and Syria launched a conventional war to attempt to recover the territories that Israel had seized from them six years earlier in the June 1967 War, the new counter-offensive launched by Hamas evokes the boldness of the biblical David in his fight against the giant Goliath. Combining rudimentary air, sea, and land means — the equivalent of David's sling — Hamas's fighters executed an amazing and highly daring offensive all along the border zone between the Gaza strip and the Israeli state.

In the same way as Israel's arrogant self-confidence in the face of its Arab neighbours was shattered in 1973, the security and impunity that it has been taking for granted in dealing with the Palestinian people and combatting Palestinian guerrillas have been severely and irreversibly impaired. From that angle, Hamas's October counter-offensive is to the Israeli population and state a powerful reminder of their vulnerability and of the fact that there can be no security without peace and no peace without justice.

Whatever one may think of Hamas's decision to launch such a massive operation against the Israeli state, thus inevitably unleashing the Israeli government's massive murderous retaliation and inciting it to attempt to wipe off Hamas and its allies from the Gaza Strip at a huge cost for civilians, the fact remains that this counter-offensive has already and undoubtedly dealt a heavy blow to the unbearable haughtiness of the Israeli racist far-right government and their belief that Israel could ever reach a "normal" state of coexistence with its regional environment while persecuting the Palestinian people and inflicting upon them a protracted Nakba of territorial dispossession, ethnic cleansing and apartheid.

No less unbearable is the precipitation with which Western governments (and a Ukrainian government that ought to know better about the legitimate fight against foreign occupation) have expressed their solidarity with Israel, very much in contrast with their muted reactions to Israel's brutal onslaughts on the Palestinian population. The Israeli flag was projected on Berlin's Brandenburg Gate on the evening of 7 October in a contemptible display of fawning over the state of Israel, the usual hallmark of German misoriented redemption-seeking for Nazi crimes against European Jews by endorsing Israel's crimes against the Palestinians. This becomes even worse at a time when Israel's government is composed of the whole gamut of Jewish far-right forces, including people whom a prominent Israeli Holocaust historian did not hesitate to aptly describe in Haaretz as neo-Nazis![1]

No less contemptible are the attempts at "analysing" Hamas's offensive as an Iranian plot to derail the ongoing US-fostered rapprochement between the Saudi kingdom and the Israeli state. Even if it were true that Tehran wishes to derail that rapprochement instead of using it to enhance its own claim of monopoly over anti-Zionism, a very disputable hypothesis indeed, this denial of Palestinian agency by way of conspiracy theory is the exact equivalent of every oppressive government's reaction to popular revolt. It postulates that there are no sufficient grounds for the oppressed people to revolt against their oppression and that any such move is necessarily inspired by the invisible hand of some foreign government.

Anyone familiar with what the Palestinian people has been enduring for decades, and aware of the kind of open air prison that the Gaza Strip has become, ever since it was occupied in 1967 and then evacuated by Israeli troops in 2005—an open air prison that is periodically the target of a murderous Israeli "turkey shoot"—can easily understand that the only reason why such quasi-desperate act of bravery as Hamas's latest operation does not actually happen more frequently is the huge military disproportion between the Palestinian David and the Israeli Goliath. Gaza's latest counter-offensive brings indeed to mind the 1943 Warsaw Ghetto Uprising.[2]

There can be no doubt that this new chapter will end with a terrible cost for the Palestinians in general, the Gazans in particular, and Hamas specifically—much higher than the cost endured by the Israelis, as has unfailingly been the case in every round of fighting between Israel and the Palestinians. And whereas it is not difficult to understand the "enough-is-enough" logic behind Hamas's counter-offensive, it is much more doubtful that it will help advance the Palestinian cause beyond the blow to Israel's self-confidence mentioned above. This would have been achieved at a hugely disproportionate cost for the Palestinians.

The very idea that such an operation, however spectacular it was, could achieve "victory" can only stem from the religious type of magical thinking

that is characteristic of a fundamentalist movement like Hamas. The distribution by its information service of a video showing the movement's
leadership praying to thank God on the morning
of 7 October is a good illustration of this thinking. Unfortunately, no magic can alter the fact of
Israel's massive military superiority: the result of
Israel's new ongoing war against Gaza is certainly
going to be devastating.

The 9/11 attacks on New York and Washington dealt the United States' arrogance a spectacular blow. Eventually, they tremendously enhanced
George W. Bush's popularity and enabled him to
launch 18 months later the occupation of Iraq
that he ambitioned. Likewise, Hamas's October
counter-offensive has already succeeded in reunify-
ing a previously deeply divided Israeli society and
polity, and it will allow Benjamin Netanyahu to
implement his wildest plans to inflict massive terror on the Palestinians to precipitate their forced
displacement.

On the other hand, if Hamas's leadership had
been betting on Lebanon's Hezbollah—and Iran
behind it—to join the war at a level that would

really put Israel in jeopardy, this bet would be very risky indeed. For not only it is far from certain that Hezbollah would take the high risk of massively entering a new war with Israel, but such a situation, if it were to happen, would inevitably bring Israel to resort unrestrainedly to its massive destructive power (which includes nuclear weapons), thus bringing about a catastrophe of historic magnitude.

Against an oppressor that is far superior in military means, the only truly efficient way of struggle for the Palestinian people is by choosing the terrain on which they can circumvent that superiority. The peak in Palestinian's struggle effectiveness was reached in the year 1988 during the First Intifada, in which the Palestinians deliberately avoided the use of violent means. This led to a deep moral crisis in Israel's society and polity, including its armed forces, and was a key factor in leading the Israeli Rabin-Peres leadership to negotiate the 1993 Oslo Accords with Yasir Arafat—however flawed these accords were, due to the Palestinian leader's indulging in wishful thinking.

The Palestinian struggle must rely primarily

on mass political action against Israel's oppression, occupation, and settler-colonial expansion. The new underground armed resistance organised by young Palestinians in Jenin or Nablus can be an efficient adjuvant to the people's mass movement, provided it is predicated on the latter's priority and conceived in such a way as to incentivise it. The regional support that the Palestinian people should rely upon is not that of tyrannical governments like that of Iran, but that of the peoples fighting against these oppressive regimes. Herein lies the true potential prospect for Palestinian liberation, which needs to be combined with the emancipation of Israeli society itself from the logic of Zionism that has inexorably produced its polity's ever-expanding drift to the far right.

8 October 2023

2

The impending catastrophe and the urgency of stopping it

In the last few days, Gaza has epitomized the global North-South divide more than any other conflict in contemporary history. The indecent unanimity of Western governments in unreservedly expressing their unconditional support of the Israeli state — at the very moment when the latter had already and quite obviously embarked on a campaign of war crimes against the Palestinian people of unprecedented magnitude in the 75-year-long history of the regional conflict — has been truly sickening. Since 7 October, these governments have been outbidding each other in this endeavour — from projecting the Israeli flag on Berlin's Brandenburg Gate, London's Parliament, Paris's Eiffel Tower and Washington's White House, to sending military hardware to Israel as well as dispatching U.S. and UK naval reinforcements to the Eastern Mediterranean in a gesture of solidarity with the Zionist state, to prohibiting diverse forms of expression of political support to the Palestinian cause, thus curtailing elementary political freedoms.

All this is happening at a time when the usual imbalance in Western media reporting on Israel/ Palestine has reached a peak. As usual, grieving Israelis, women in particular, have been profusely shown on screens, incomparably more than grieving Palestinians have ever been. Hamas's Operation Al-Aqsa Flood occasioned a flood of images of violence against unarmed people, with a special focus on a rave similar to those commonly organized in Western countries, so as to accentuate the "narcissistic compassion ... evoked much more by calamities striking 'people like us', much less by calamities affecting people unlike us."[3] The much larger-scale Israeli violence that has been pounding civilians in Gaza since Hamas launched its operation has been much less reported, let alone condemned. Even as blatant a war crime as the total blockade in water, food, fuel, and electricity inflicted upon a population of 2.3 million and the no less blatant violation of humanitarian law consisting in ordering more than one million civilians to leave their city or face death under the rubbles of their dwellings is all but condoned by prominent Western political leaders and major Western media.

It is as if they had reconstituted the International Society for the Suppression of Savage Customs for which Joseph Conrad's fictional Kurtz (in *Heart of Darkness*) had written a report ending with the terrifying postscript: "Exterminate all the brutes!" Kurtz's prescription has indeed found an equivalent in Israeli minister of "defence" Yoav Gallant's sinister announcement: "I have ordered a complete siege on the Gaza Strip. There will be no electricity, no food, no fuel, everything is closed ... We are fighting human animals and we are acting accordingly."[4]

Western media have been unsurprisingly echoing Israel's media in depicting Hamas's operation as the deadliest attack targeting Jews since the Holocaust, continuing the usual pattern of Nazification of the Palestinians in order to justify their dehumanization and extermination. The truth, though, is that, however dreadful some aspects of Hamas's operation have been, they are not a continuation of Nazi imperialist violence in any meaningful historical perspective. They are inscribed instead in two very different historical cycles: that of the Palestinians' struggle against Israeli colonial dispossession and oppression, and that of the struggle of the peoples of the Global South against colonialism. The key to the mindset behind Hamas's action is not to be found in Adolf Hitler's *Mein Kampf*, but indeed in Frantz Fanon's *Wretched of the Earth* — the best-known interpretation of the feelings of the colonized by a political thinker who was also a psychiatrist. Fanon reflected on the struggles of the colonized against French colonialism — the Algerians in particular. The parallels are striking:

The colonized, who have made up their mind to make such an agenda into a driving force, have been prepared for violence from time immemorial. As soon as they are born it is obvious to them that their cramped world, riddled with taboos, can only be challenged by out and out violence. ...

The violence which governed the ordering of the colonial world ... will be vindicated and appropriated when, taking history into their own hands, the colonized swarm into the forbidden cities. To blow the colonial world to smithereens is henceforth a clear image within the grasp and imagination of every colonized subject. ...

The outcome, however, is profoundly unequal, for machinegunning by planes or bombardments from naval vessels outweigh in horror and scope the response from the colonized. The most alienated of the colonized are once and for all demystified by this pendulum motion of terror and counterterror. They see for themselves that any number of speeches on human equality cannot mask the absurdity whereby seven Frenchmen killed or wounded in an ambush at the Sakamody pass sparks the indignation of civilized consciences, whereas the sacking of the Guergour douars, the Djerah dechra, and the massacre of the population behind the ambush count for nothing.

Were some of the acts committed by Hamas fighters during Operation Al-Aqsa Flood "terroristic"? If by "terrorism" is meant the deliberate assassination of unarmed people, they certainly were. But then, the deliberate killing of thousands upon thousands of Gazan civilians over the past seventeen years — since 2006, a few months only after Israel evacuated the Gaza Strip to control it from without, in the belief that the cost would be lesser than controlling it from within — that is terrorism too. State terrorism has indeed caused much more casualties in history than terrorism by non-state groups.

Likewise, were some of the acts committed by Hamas fighters acts of "barbarism"? Undoubtedly so, but they were no less undoubtedly part of a

clash of barbarisms.[5] Allow me to quote here from
what I wrote about this more than twenty years
ago, in the wake of the 9/11 attacks:

> Taken separately, each barbarous act can be
> judged equally reprehensible from a moral
> standpoint. No civilized ethic can justify de-
> liberate assassination of non-combatants or
> children, whether indiscriminate or deliber-
> ate, by state or non-governmental terror. ...
>
> Nevertheless, from the point of view of
> basic fairness, we cannot wrap ourselves in
> a metaphysical ethic that rejects all forms of
> barbarism equally. The different barbarisms
> do not carry the same weight in the scales of
> justice. Admittedly, barbarism can never be
> an instrument of "legitimate self-defence";
> it is always illegitimate by definition. But
> this does not change the fact that when two
> barbarisms clash, the stronger, the one that
> acts as the oppressor, is still the more culpa-
> ble. Except in cases of manifest irrationality,
> the barbarism of the weak is most often,
> logically enough, a reaction to the barbarism

of the strong. Otherwise, why would the weak provoke the strong, at the risk of being crushed themselves? This is, incidentally, why the strong seek to hide their culpability by portraying their adversaries as demented, demonic and bestial.

The most crucial issue with Hamas's conception of the fight against Israeli occupation and oppression is not moral, but political and practical. Instead of serving Palestinian emancipation and winning over to its cause an increasing number of Israelis, Hamas's strategy[6] facilitates the nationalist unity of Jewish Israelis and provides the Zionist state with pretexts for increased suppression of Palestinian rights and existence. The idea that the Palestinian people could achieve its national emancipation by way of armed confrontation with an Israeli state that is far superior militarily is irrational. The most effective episode in Palestinian struggle to this day was unarmed: The 1988 Intifada provoked a deep crisis in Israel's society, polity, and armed forces, and won for the Palestinian cause massive sympathy in the world, Western countries included.

Hamas's latest operation, the most spectacular attack it ever launched on Israel, has provided an opportunity for much more than the usual pattern of brutal murderous retaliation in a protracted cycle of violence and counter-violence. What looms on the horizon is nothing less than a second stage of the Nakba — the Arabic word for "catastrophe" that is the name given to the forced displacement of most of the indigenous Palestinian population from the territories that the newborn Israeli state managed to conquer in 1948. The present Israeli government, which includes neo-Nazis,[7] is led by the leader of Likud and heir, therefore, of the political groups that perpetrated the most infamous massacre of Palestinians in 1948: the Deir Yassin massacre.[8] Benjamin Netanyahu led the opposition to Ariel Sharon and resigned from the Israeli cabinet run by the latter in 2005, when Sharon opted for Israel's "unilateral disengagement"[9] from Gaza. Soon after, Sharon quitted Likud which Netanyahu has been leading ever since.

The Israeli far right led by Likud has been

relentlessly pursuing its goal of a Greater Israel that encompasses the entire territory of British-mandate Palestine between the Mediterranean Sea and the Jordan River, including both the West Bank and Gaza. Only a few days before Hamas's operation, Netanyahu, during his speech at the UN[10] General Assembly, brandished a map of Greater Israel — a deliberate signal that did not go unnoticed. That is why the injunction given to the population of Northern Gaza to move southward is much more than the usual hypocritical excuse for the deliberate destruction of civilian-populated areas, while laying the blame at Hamas's door by accusing it of hiding among civilians (an absurd accusation indeed: how could Hamas exist in the wilderness, out of urban concentrations, without being wiped off by far superior Israeli remote warfare means?).

What we are witnessing is in all likelihood the prelude to a second round of displacement of Gazans toward the Egyptian Sinai, in the intention of committing the second major act of territorial conquest combined with ethnic cleansing since the Nakba, under the pretext of eradicating

Hamas. The Palestinians immediately remembered the 1948 exodus, when they fled war only to be prevented from returning to their towns and villages. They have understood that they are now facing in Gaza a second instance of forced displacement preluding to further dispossession and settler-colonization. This second stage of the Nakba will be much bloodier than the first: The number of Palestinians killed until the time of writing is already nearing the number of those killed in 1948, and this is but the beginning of the Israeli onslaught. Only massive popular mobilization in the United States and Europe to bring Western governments to pressure Israel into stopping before it fulfils its sinister war aims could prevent this dreadful outcome. This is extremely urgent. Make no mistake: the impending catastrophe will not be contained in the Middle East but will certainly spill over into Western countries as has been happening for several decades — on a yet more tragic scale.

16 October 2023

3

Two Gaza scenarios: Greater Israel vs. Oslo

Announced as imminent several days ago, after over 1 million inhabitants of the northern half of the Gaza Strip were given only 24 hours to flee south, the Israeli armed forces' land onslaught on Gaza is yet to start at the time of writing. Despite attempts to convey a contrary impression, this delay reflects the fact that Israel's political leadership and military command had no oven-ready plan for the invasion of Gaza on the scale they have been contemplating since the assault launched by Hamas on

7 October. The Israeli armed forces could hardly have been anticipating a reoccupation of Gaza, which they evacuated 18 years ago. The successive operations they launched against the strip in 2006, 2008-09, 2012, 2014 and 2021 — to mention only the largest ones — have all been limited, essentially consisting of bombing, along with limited ground assaults in 2009 and 2014. But the extraordinary scale and traumatising effect of 7 October made it impossible for Israel's leaders to set a lesser goal than the total eradication of Hamas from Gaza and the "pacification" of the strip.

This is a formidable challenge, for not only does the invasion of such a densely populated territory involve urban warfare of a kind that is highly risky for the assailant, but it poses most acutely the problem of what to do with the conquered territory the day after. The issue is not only military, needless to say; it is also, even primarily, political. The tight interdependency of political and military considerations is especially clear in the present situation. The scale of violence that is unavoidable in the pursuit of Israel's proclaimed goals will inevitably provoke a political fallout, which will impact the conduct of the war itself.

The most obvious factor in the equation is that Israel's tolerance for losses among its troops is very limited, as illustrated most spectacularly by the exchange in 2011 of Israeli soldier Gilad Shalit, held captive in Gaza, for over 1,000 Palestinian prisoners. This makes it impossible for the Israeli army to launch ground assaults under conditions that impose a heavy cost in soldiers' lives, like the assaults that Russian troops (regular ones and/or those affiliated with the Wagner paramilitary service) have been launching in Ukraine since 2022 — not to mention extreme cases like Iran's "human waves" during its 1980-88 war with Iraq. Thus, the Israeli army's superiority is at its maximum in terrains such as Egypt's Sinai desert or the Syrian Golan Heights, where buildings are scarce and firepower from a distance is decisive. Conversely, when Ariel Sharon, Israel's minister of defense at the time, ordered his troops to enter besieged Beirut in early August 1982, they had to abandon the attempt the next day. It was only after the negotiated evacuation of Palestinian fighters from Beirut that

Israeli forces managed to storm the city in mid-September. They withdrew by the end of the same month after a nascent Lebanese urban resistance movement started targeting them.

A corollary of this is that the only way for Israel's army to invade any part of so dense and vast an urban landscape as the Gaza Strip with minimal Israeli losses is to flatten the areas that it strives to occupy by way of intensive bombing before launching the ground offensive. This is indeed what started in the immediate aftermath of 7 October, with a level of damage that, in both extent and intensity, goes way beyond prior Israeli bombing campaigns, from Lebanon in 2006 to the successive wars on Gaza. Flattening vast swaths of urban territory was not possible for the Israeli military in any of the previous wars — not for lack of destructive power, of course, but for the absence of the necessary political conditions.

This was most obvious in 1982, when the Israeli siege of Beirut provoked a major international outcry and political crisis inside Israel itself, where the opposition to the Likud government of Menachem Begin and Ariel Sharon came out in massive protests. In the previous wars against Gaza, Israel's armed forces had no intention of reoccupying part of Gaza anyway. This time around, this intention is on clear display, and the shockwaves from the unprecedented killing of huge numbers of Israeli civilians as well as soldiers are of such a magnitude that both the Israeli public and Israel's traditional international backers are explicitly or implicitly approving the reoccupation of Gaza in its entirety. What can the eradication of Hamas and the analogy with the Islamic State group mean, short of conducting a search and sweep operation in the whole of the strip?

As the *Financial Times* recently reported, based on interviews with military experts:

> Israel's army will deploy its so-called "doctrine of victory", which requires the air force to have a deep bank of pre-vetted targets destroyed in rapid order. It is already in play, with fighter jets intensely bombing large swaths of Gaza, pausing only to refuel, often in mid-air. The campaign is meant to outpace the ability of Hamas to regroup

and, according to a person familiar with the discussions that created the 2020 doctrine, to "achieve maximum goals before the international community puts political pressure to slow down".

This is the military scenario that is brewing. Now comes the political dimension. If the military goal is indeed to reoccupy Gaza in order to eradicate Hamas, the next questions, naturally, are: For how long, and to replace Hamas with what? There is much more room for disagreement on these two questions of political strategy than on the military strategy, whose parameters are much narrower since they depend on objective considerations and the nature of the military means at hand. The two opposite poles of the political divergence translate into two scenarios that we might call the Greater Israel scenario and the Oslo scenario.

The Greater Israel scenario is the one that appeals most to Benjamin Netanyahu and his acolytes on Israel's far right. The Likud Party is heir to the Zionist far right, known as Revisionist Zionism, whose armed offshoots perpetrated the Deir

Yassin massacre, the most infamous mass murder of Palestinians in 1948, amid what the Arabs call the Nakba (catastrophe). On the 78% of the territory of British Mandate Palestine that Zionist armed forces managed to conquer during the war of that year (the Zionists had been granted 55% by the partition plan approved by a nascent United Nations Organization, then dominated by countries of the Global North), 80% of the Palestinian population were uprooted. They had fled the war, frightened by atrocities such as Deir Yassin, and were never to be allowed to return to their homes and land. And yet the Zionist far right never forgave mainstream Zionism, which was then led by David Ben-Gurion, for having agreed to stop the war before conquering 100% of British Mandate Palestine between the Mediterranean Sea and the Jordan River.

During his recent speech at the U.N. General Assembly in New York, only two weeks before 7 October, Netanyahu brandished a map of the Middle East showing a Greater Israel that included Gaza and the West Bank. Even more relevant to the new Gaza war is the fact — hardly mentioned in the global media — that Netanyahu had resigned from the Israeli cabinet led by Sharon in 2005 in protest against the latter's decision to withdraw from Gaza. (Sharon had succeeded Netanyahu as the head of Likud in 1999, following the latter's electoral defeat to the Labor Party then led by Ehud Barak. Sharon then managed to win the next election, in 2003, and offered the ministry of finance to Netanyahu.)

Much more an army man than a politician, Sharon was attentive to the military's plea for a withdrawal of troops from the unruly Gaza, with a preference for controlling the strip from outside. He saw no prospect for an annexation of Gaza similar to what has been occurring in the West Bank since its occupation in 1967. He therefore judged that it would be wiser to let the Palestinian Authority, established by the 1993 Oslo Accords, take care of Gaza, while focusing on the West Bank — a much more prized and consensual Zionist goal.

Oslo required the withdrawal of Israeli troops only from those West Bank areas densely populated by Palestinians, while allowing Israel to maintain control of most of the territory. To show his contempt for the Palestinian Authority, Sharon opted for a unilateral "disengagement" from Gaza in 2005 — without preparing it with the Palestinian Authority, that is. Two years later, Hamas seized power in the strip.

Netanyahu protested Sharon's disengagement. He led the opposition to Sharon within Likud and gathered enough force to incite him to quit the party and found a new one that same year, 2005. Netanyahu has led Likud ever since. He maneuvered his way to the prime ministership in 2009 by playing on the fragmentation of the Israeli political scene — an art at which, as the consummate opportunist, he excels — and remained in office until June 2021. By the end of 2022, he was back at the helm, heading the most far-right government in Israel's history — a country where several successive governments since Likud's first victory in 1977 have been labelled the "most right-wing in history" in an unending drift to the right. Netanyahu nodded to Donald Trump's (and Jared Kushner's) "peace plan" in 2020 only because he knew full well that the Palestinians could not accept it. He likely saw this inevitable rejection as a good pretext for a unilateral annexation of most of the West Bank at some later point.

The prospect of reconquering Gaza required a major upheaval that was not on the horizon. No one could have expected that it would be created, all of a sudden, by Hamas' "Al-Aqsa Flood" operation. It was indeed the Israeli equivalent of 9/11. 7 October was in fact 20 times more deadly than 9/11 relative to each country's population, as Netanyahu pointed out to Joe Biden during the latter's visit to Israel on 18 October. Just as 9/11 created the political conditions that allowed the Bush administration to realise its pet project of invading Iraq, Israel's 7 October created the political conditions for Gaza's reconquest, something that Netanyahu had long desired but that was too wild and out of bounds to be openly discussed up to that point. Whether this goal is attainable remains to be seen, of course, but it is what the Zionist hard right aspires to.

The repeated calls by Israel's political and military authorities to Gaza's inhabitants to flee southward toward the border with Egypt, and their eagerness to convince Cairo to open the door to the Sinai Peninsula and take in the bulk of Gaza's population (2.3 million people), are thus rightly understood by the Egyptians as an invitation to let the Gazans settle in Sinai for the indefinite future — just as the Palestinians displaced from their land in 1948 and 1967 have been turned into permanent refugees in neighbouring Arab countries. On 18 October, Egyptian President Abdel Fattah el-Sisi poured cold water on this idea, cunningly advising Israel to give refuge to the Gazans in the Negev desert, within its own 1948 territory, if it is truly seeking to grant them only temporary shelter.

Greater Israel is not a unanimous ambition of Israel's leaders, however — not even after 7 October. It has some support in the United States, from the far right of the Republican Party and among Christian Zionists. But it is certainly not supported by the bulk of the U.S. foreign policy establishment, the Democrats in particular. The Biden administration — well known to have little sympathy for Netanyahu, who in 2012 openly backed Mitt Romney for president against Barack Obama (and Biden, his vice president) — sticks to the prospect, created by the Oslo Accords, of a

Palestinian rump state, providing an alibi to side-line the Palestinian cause and clear the way for the development of links and collaboration between Israel and the Arab states.

This is why Biden told CBS on 15 October that "it would be a big mistake" for Israel to occupy Gaza. The U.S. president did not mean that the invasion of the entire strip in order to eradicate Hamas would be a mistake. On the contrary, he clearly stated that, "Going in but taking out the extremists ... is a necessary requirement." Asked then "Do you believe that Hamas must be eliminated entirely?" Biden replied:

Yes, I do. But there needs to be a Palestinian authority. There needs to be a path to a Palestinian state. That path, called "the two state solution," has been U.S. policy for decades. It would create an independent nation next to Israel for 5 million Palestinians who live in Gaza and on the West Bank of the Jordan River.

The purpose of Biden's daylong visit to Israel was not only to enhance his political profile for the 2024 presidential election, ensuring that Trump, right-wing Republicans and evangelical Christian

Zionists can't outflank him in their military support for Israel. (Note that in so doing, Biden is going against the views of a majority of U.S. citizens, and especially the majority of Democrats, who favour a more balanced approach to the Israeli-Palestinian conflict.) Nor was Biden's purpose only to negotiate a token humanitarian gesture in order to pretend that his administration is doing all it can to alleviate the unfolding disaster. His purpose was also, and perhaps primarily, to convince the Israeli polity — with or without Netanyahu — of the necessity of sticking to the Oslo perspective. He aimed to boost this endeavour by meeting with Mahmoud Abbas, the head of the Palestinian Authority, and with the king of Jordan. But the destruction of the Al-Ahli Arab Hospital on the eve of his visit thwarted his plan.

The clearest indication yet that part of the Israeli military-political establishment sees eye to eye with the Biden administration has been provided by Ehud Barak, former chief of the general staff of the Israeli armed forces and former prime minister. He fine-tuned the Oslo scenario in an interview with The Economist:

Mr Barak believes that the optimal outcome, once Hamas's military capabilities have been sufficiently degraded, is the re-establishment of the Palestinian Authority in Gaza. ... However he warns that Mahmoud Abbas, the Palestinian president, "cannot be seen to be returning on Israeli bayonets". There will, therefore, need to be an interim period during which "Israel will capitulate to international pressure and hand Gaza over to an Arab peacekeeping force, which could include members such as Egypt, Morocco and the United Arab Emirates. They would secure the area until the Palestinian Authority could take control."

The fact that the Oslo process stalled shortly after being launched with great pomp and circumstance in 1993 — which led to the outbreak of the Second Intifada in 2000, followed by Israel's temporary reoccupation of those parts of the West Bank that it had evacuated in favour of the Palestinian Authority — does not seem to deter Washington and its allies from regarding it as the only feasible settlement. They probably believe that some sort of territorial swap like the one that was envisaged in the Trump-Kushner "peace

plan" might eventually square the circle of recon-
ciling the annexation of the West Bank areas where
settlements have been proliferating with granting
the Palestinians a fragmented "independent state"
on 22% of their ancestral land west of the Jordan
River.

Ultimately, the two scenarios — Greater Israel
and Oslo — are predicated on Israel's ability to
destroy Hamas to a degree sufficient to prevent it
from controlling Gaza. This entails the conquest
of most of the strip, if not all of it, by Israel's
armed forces — a goal they could only achieve by
destroying most of Gaza, which would come at an
enormous human cost.

The *Washington Post* recently quoted Bruce
Hoffman, a counterterrorism expert and professor
at Georgetown University, who pointed to the
eradication of the Tamil Tigers in the northern part
of Sri Lanka as the only type of success achievable
in such endeavours. The Tigers were wiped out in
2009 after a military offensive by Sri Lanka's armed
forces that involved the killing of up to 40,000
civilians, according to U.N. estimates. "God forbid
that that sort of carnage unfolds today," Hoffman

told the Post. "But, if you're determined to destroy a terrorist organization, you can. There's a ruthlessness that goes with it."

Except that the world's attention is incomparably more focused on what happens in the Middle East than it was on what happened in Sri Lanka. The question therefore becomes what the Israeli army can achieve before a combination of losses in personnel and international pressure forces it to stop, not to mention the possibility of a regional conflagration involving Lebanon's Hezbollah, with Iran backing it. So it is by no means certain that either of the two scenarios will materialize. Israel's military has cautiously drafted a minimal plan consisting of creating a new extended buffer zone inside Gaza all along its borders, further aggravating the strip's condition as an "open-air prison."

The only thing that is certain is that Israel's new onslaught on Gaza is already deadlier and more destructive than all previous episodes in the tragic 75-year history of the Israeli-Palestinian conflict. It's also certain that this is going to get exponentially worse, which will only add to the destabilization of what is already the most unstable region of the world, and which plays a major role in destabilizing the Global North itself — with waves of refugees and the spillover of violence. Yet again, the short-sightedness and double standards of the United States and its European allies are going to blow back in their faces — this time with even more tragic consequences.

23 October 2023

4

The Plan to Complete the Nakba Revealed

A document leaked in recent days has fully confirmed what we have been warning of since 7 October, which is that the Zionist right will seize the opportunity of Operation "Al-Aqsa Flood" to try to implement its old dream of displacing most of the Palestinian population from the territories occupied in 1967, so as to complete the 1948 Nakba and achieve their "Greater Israel" project. On Saturday 28 October, the Israeli opposition website "Mecomit" (Local Call) published an important document issued by the Zionist Ministry of Intelligence, headed by Gila Gamliel, a prominent member of the Likud Party led by Benjamin Netanyahu. The document's authenticity was later confirmed by a few Israeli media outlets, including *Haaretz* on Monday 30 October, and it was translated into English by the +972 website, which is critical of Israel.

The document dated 13 October is entitled "Options for a policy regarding Gaza's civilian population." The three options envisaged are: (a) The residents of Gaza remain in the Strip and are governed by the Palestinian Authority; (b) The population of Gaza remain in the Strip and a local Arab authority is established there; (c) The civilian population is evacuated from Gaza to Sinai. The document considers that options (a) and (b) suffer from significant deficiencies, especially in that neither of them can provide a sufficient "deterrent effect" in the long term. As for option (c), the document asserts that it "will yield positive, long-term strategic outcomes for Israel," and it is "executable." "It requires determination from the political echelon in the face of international pressure, with an emphasis on harnessing the support of the United States and additional pro-Israeli countries for the endeavor."

The document then goes on to detail each of the three options. We will limit ourselves here to the third option favored by the Ministry, which is the option of evacuating the civilian population from Gaza. The document describes the scenario as follows: "1. Due to the fighting against Hamas, there is a need to evacuate the non-combatant population from the combat area; 2. Israel should act to evacuate the civilian population to Sinai; 3. In the first stage, tent cities will be established in the area of Sinai, the next stage includes the establishment of a humanitarian zone to assist the civilian population of Gaza and the construction of cities in a resettled area in northern Sinai; 4. A buffer zone of several kilometers should be created within Egypt, and the return of the population to activities/residences near the border with Israel should not be allowed. In addition, a security perimeter should be established in our territory near the border with Egypt."

The document then details the displacement

scenario, which begins with a call for the evacuation of non-combatants from the combat zone, and the implementation of focused air strikes on northern Gaza to make way for a ground invasion. In a second phase, the invasion begins from the north and along the border until the entire Gaza Strip is occupied and Hamas tunnels are eliminated. Throughout this time, "it is important to leave the travel routes to the south open to enable the evacuation of the civilian population toward Rafah." The document claims that this option would save civilian lives compared to the other two options, and that it falls within a global context of large-scale displacement as in Syria, Afghanistan, and Ukraine. It believes that it is Egypt's duty under international law to make way for the passage of the civilian population, and that Cairo, in return for its cooperation, will receive financial assistance to alleviate its current economic crisis.

It is noteworthy that the document of the Zionist Ministry of Intelligence was issued at the time when Israel started calling on the residents of northern Gaza to immigrate to the south of the Wadi Gaza River on 13 October, a confirmation that this call conformed with option (C). As a matter of fact, everything Israel has done so far is completely consistent with the plan for a repetition of the Nakba in Gaza, as described in the document. The *Financial Times* published a report on Monday 30 October by its correspondents in European capitals stating that Netanyahu sought to persuade European governments to pressure Cairo in order to convince Egypt to take in refugees coming from Gaza. Paris, Berlin, and London all expressed their conviction that this demand is unrealistic, but they nevertheless started putting pressure on Cairo to open the doors of Egypt, citing humanitarian considerations. It appears from the report that there is a belief in some European circles that the sheer size of displacement to the Egyptian border, increasing with the progress of ground military operations, would exacerbate the concentration of people on the border to a point that, in conjunction with Western pressure, may force Egypt to change its position. The displacement planners must also certainly hope that the crowd of displaced people on the southern Gaza border will manage to storm into Egyptian territory to escape Israel's bombing and military advance, thus forcing themselves upon the Egyptian authorities who will not be able to fire on Gazan civilians.

Meanwhile, settlers in the West Bank, for their part, have begun seizing the opportunity of the "Al-Aqsa Flood" to escalate the pressure on the Palestinians living in Area "C" (which includes the largest portion of the West Bank's lands – more than 60 percent) calling on them to migrate, not to the area supervised by the "Palestinian Authority" but to Jordan! This clearly indicates the Zionist right's intention to complete the Nakba throughout the West Bank as well, as soon as the opportunity arises in their view.

31 October 2023

5

The Zionist Genocidal War and its Accomplices

We sometimes hear from those who wish to mitigate the impact of what the State of Israel has been doing since Operation Al-Aqsa Flood that it was committing daily crimes and waging periodic wars anyway, so that its new onslaught on Gaza is nothing but a continuation of this old, permanent pattern. It is true, of course, that crime and aggression are two fundamental pillars of the Zionist state as a settler-colonial state based on war and "ethnic cleansing". Nevertheless, downplaying the current aggression against Gaza and denying that it is qualitatively distinct from all previous tragedies that the people of Palestine have suffered since the Nakba until this day, converges with the fallacies that the Zionists and their supporters are trying to spread in pretending that the death toll numbers coming from Gaza are exaggerated for the purpose of propaganda.

The truth is that the current aggression against Gaza constitutes, in the clearest possible form, a genocidal war that includes mass murder and "ethnic cleansing", two crimes against humanity in the classification of international law. These crimes exceed qualitatively everything committed by the Zionist armed forces since 1949 until today and are comparable to what happened during the Nakba. They even exceed the latter in terms of intensity of killing, destruction, and displacement. The Nakba of 1947-1949 was a war aimed at seizing the land of Palestine and practicing "ethnic cleansing" over it, whereby the overwhelming majority of the population of the occupied territory were turned into refugees, while a number of them estimated at more than 11,000 were killed, out of approximately 1.3 million of Arab inhabitants of Palestine at that time.

As for the current aggression against Gaza, it has so far, in less than seven weeks, caused approximately 15,000 deaths, at the very least, out of approximately 2.4 million inhabitants of the Gaza Strip, with more than half of them displaced from the north of the strip to its south in preparation for their displacement out of Palestine, as far-right Zionist circles wish, or at least their gathering on the Egyptian border in refugee camps that would serve as concentration camps under the supervision of the Israeli army. And these are only the results of the first phase of the Zionist aggression, which targeted the northern part of the Gaza Strip, and should be followed by a second phase focused on its southern part, which would greatly exacerbate the number of casualties.

This is happening through a killing and destruction madness that exceeds anything witnessed in the world's wars since the dropping of the atomic bombs on Japan in 1945. The matter has reached such a point that the *New York Times*[11] has revealed the horror of what is occurring, even though the US government is directly complicit in the aggression. This was in an article by Lauren Leatherby, published on 25 November, under the title, "The civilian population of Gaza, under an Israeli barrage of fire, is being killed at a historic rate". The author of the report explained that the issue is not only related to the pace of the bombing, which amounted to 15,000 strikes until the present truce, but also to its quality, as Israel has been extensively using 2,000-pound bombs (900 kilograms), rarely used since World War II and the Korean and Vietnam wars.

The report quotes US military officials as saying that they have almost never used such a calibre in the present century, and that they have avoided using even 500-pound bombs because they are too large to be dropped on populated urban areas, such as Mosul in Iraq or Raqqa in Syria during the war against ISIS. During the battle of Mosul, which began in October 2016 and lasted nine months, about 10,000 people were killed between victims of ISIS and victims of the US-led international coalition, that is, two-thirds of the number of those killed by the Israeli campaign in Gaza in less than seven weeks.

What makes these numbers even more dangerous and horrific is that about 70% of those claimed by the Zionist genocidal machine in Gaza are women and children, a huge percentage unparalleled in any contemporary war. The *New York Times* report states that the number of children who died under the barrage of Israeli bombs in Gaza during the past seven weeks exceeds the total number of children killed last year in all the wars taking place in various global arenas, including the Ukraine war that began in February 2022.

Another report published by the *Washington Post*[12] on 13th November stated that the number of children killed by Israel in Gaza during the first month of its insane bombing exceeded the number of children killed in the wars in Yemen and Iraq, and amounted to a third of the number of children killed during ten years of war in Syria. The newspaper compared the 4,125 children killed in Gaza in one month with the following average numbers of children killed in one month of fighting in Iraq (19), Yemen (41), Afghanistan (56), and Syria

(100). It is no secret that the killing of children, in particular, is a blatant feature of genocide as it expresses the will to annihilate the targeted people.

All of these data demonstrate the great gravity of the genocidal war waged by the Zionist state against the people of Gaza since Operation Al-Aqsa Flood. This is not surprising, as the extreme thirst of revenge generated among Israeli Jews combined with the presence of the Zionist far right in power, made such insane violence very predictable. The matter was easy to anticipate, and hence the gravity of the support lent by Western governments to the Zionist onslaught under the pretext of Israel's alleged right to "self-defence" (the number of those it has killed so far has exceeded ten times those it lost as a result of Al-Aqsa Flood) —a support that went as far as rejecting the call for a ceasefire, in addition to the United States, Germany, and others sending military reinforcements to Israel and to the eastern Mediterranean in support of Israel's onslaught — is truly immense. This is the first time since the middle of the past century that these governments have openly supported a genocidal war. What is even more serious is the complicity of the governments of Arab countries, which have so far refrained from weaponizing oil despite their awareness that it constitutes the strongest means of pressure in their possession that can help the people of Palestine. That is because Western countries today fear the return of oil prices to the rise, not only for economic reasons but also and primarily because this would serve Russia's interest in financing its war on Ukraine, at a time when it is facing difficulties in this regard.

28 November 2023

6

The crisis in Gaza: an interview

This interview was conducted on 16 January 2009 for *Irish Left Review*, towards the end of Israel's assault on Gaza, also known as Operation Cast Lead. This Gaza War started on 27 December 2008 and ended on18 January 2009 resulting in the death of 1,400 Palestinian and 13 Israelis. The Israeli armed forces claimed that the aim of Operation Cast Lead was to stop rocket fire. Israel attacked not just what it claimed were military targets, but it also bombed political and administrative buildings, and the densely populated cities of Gaza, Khan Yunis and Rafah. [Editors]

Daniel Finn: What do you think are the chief goals of Israeli strategy at present in their assault on the Gaza strip?

Gilbert Achcar: Well, that's a complicated question actually, because there are different levels involved. Seen through a wide angle, it is part of an ongoing struggle between Israel on the one hand and both Hamas and Hezbollah on the other, a struggle which reached a previous peak in 2006, when during the summer Israel was simultaneously waging a war against Gaza and another one, a major onslaught, on Lebanon. That was related to the global strategy of the Bush administration in its confrontation with Iran, with the conception prevailing in Washington that Hamas and Hezbollah are tools of the Iranian state and therefore part of an alliance of forces that should be smashed if ever US hegemony in the region as well as Israeli security is to be stabilized. It is therefore a further stage in the same ongoing war that has been unfolding for the last few years.

Now if we narrow the focus, the fact that this has been launched at this very moment, starting on the 27 of December, is of course related to shorter term political considerations: on the one hand, the Bush Administration will soon be out of the scene and although the Israeli government have no real reason to fear a major change in US policy in the Middle East, if we judge from all the signs given by the Obama team, there remains the prospect that the new Administration will get into talks with Iran, as Obama said he would during the electoral campaign. In that case, US backing for a tough stance in the confrontation with Iran might be diluted. Taking that into consideration, one reason why the campaign is being launched right now is in order to spare the next administration the need to cope from the beginning with a major crisis in the Middle East, so there was relief in the Obama team that this is done under Bush.

The problem is that the operation went on much longer than expected, as is now a recurrent pattern in Israel's aggressions: bygone indeed are the days of the "Six-Day War". Ideally for the Israeli government – and there were a lot of comments about this possibility some months ago – there should have been a strike against Iran itself before the Bush administration left the scene. However, that became impossible for a number of reasons related to the deep trouble in which the Bush administration finds itself: not only the general political weakness of a lame-duck president, but also the economic crisis, which makes any kind of military confrontation with Iran at this point something that would certainly be harmful to the interest of the global economy [this interview was conducted before the revelation by *The New York Times*[11] of the rejection by the Bush administration of a recent request by Israel of a green light for airstrikes on Iran's nuclear facilities]. Instead of these strikes against Iran that it was wishing for, Israel is attacking Hamas which it sees as a proxy for Iran.

And then there are even narrower perspectives involved which are the electoral considerations in Israel. As you know, new Israeli elections are to be held soon, and parties represented in the Israeli coalition government – Olmert and Livni's Kadima on the one hand and Ehud Barak's Labour party on the other-are facing strong competition from Likud, the far-right wing of the mainstream Zionist scene in Israel. In a sense this onslaught on Gaza is a way to pre-empt the outbidding on which Netanyahu would certainly have built his electoral campaign. So, if you put all these issues into consideration, you get an overdetermination, i.e., a multiplicity of reasons for this operation to be launched right now. All the rest, the rockets launched by Hamas and all that, are just pretexts, in the same way that the abduction of 2 soldiers by Hezbollah in July 2006 was but a pretext used by Israel to launch a premeditated full-scale aggression.

Daniel Finn: The last major round of confrontation between Israel and Hamas and Hezbollah in 2006 ended in a major setback for the Israeli state and all kinds of recriminations among the political and military elites. Do you think Israel now has a realistic chance of overturning that setback and talking up a victory, or does it face another defeat?

Gilbert Achcar: Well, here lies the reason why the situation is extremely dangerous and worrying right now. Think about it: this onslaught has started on the 27th of Dec so that means we are some 2 weeks into the fighting and you have already a heavier death toll in absolute numbers than what you had in Lebanon after the first two weeks of intensive bombing. And if you take it in relative numbers, knowing that the Lebanese population is close to 3 times larger than the population of Gaza, then it is much, much more. What is very worrying and dangerous about the present situation is precisely that, because of the previous fiasco in Lebanon in the summer of 2006, Israel cannot afford another fiasco of the same kind. They cannot afford a new one, for both strategic reasons and opportunistic or short-term ones, small fry political calculations, that is.

On the one hand the Israeli state stands to lose a lot of its so-called military credibility if it faces a new fiasco, all the more so that the enemy they are facing this time, i.e., Hamas in Gaza, is certainly much weaker than what Hezbollah is and was in Lebanon. Hezbollah is certainly stronger in the Lebanese Shiite community than Hamas is in Gaza where you have a bitter contest between Hamas and the PA/Fatah, and you have a few other groups competing for the same constituency. Beyond that, of course, for very obvious reasons, Hezbollah had much more weapons than Hamas has in Gaza, which is a small strip of land surrounded from all parts and under heavy surveillance. They can smuggle some light weapons, not major weapons into Gaza whereas in Lebanon, Hezbollah could build up an important arsenal – all the more easily that it was done with Syria's backing.

So, if Israel gets into a second fiasco even against Hamas which is quite weaker than Hezbollah, then this will be seen necessarily as a major disaster, worse than the 2006 one for Israel. Not to mention, and this is the second point, the petty consideration. If the ruling coalition in Israel comes out from the present war with another fiasco, its parties won't even need to go to elections. Netanyahu would stand to smash them completely and they know that. So, they cannot afford a fiasco for these two reasons combined and this is what makes the situation very, very worrying. They might develop the syndrome of the wounded beast, getting more ferocious than they are already. The level of Israeli atrocity is increasing war after war. The 33-Day War in 2006 was already the most brutal aggression in the long history of Israeli wars, the most brutal utilization of power by Israel, carpet-bombing whole regions of Lebanon, civilian areas.

The pretext then as now is that fighters are hiding among the population. This is the most hypocritical argument: what do they want them to do, to regroup in some wasteland with signposts saying "Bomb us here"? This is preposterous. The truth is that Israel is trying to crush mass political parties, which are armed, of course, but they have to be armed because they are permanently under threat. These are armed popular movements. Most of their armed members are not professional fighters living in barracks. When you take all these aspects of the problem into consideration, there are very, very serious grounds for the mounting, increasing worries that are expressed by international humanitarian agencies.

A lot of people now sense that the population of Gaza is really under threat of massive extermination. This is not the usual kind of exaggeration, it is a sober assessment when you face such a level of violence and brutality, day after day, with more and more so-called accidents in which concentrations of civilians are targeted with mass-murder as

GILBERT ACHCAR

a result. The only alternative to a fiasco for Israel is to push forward its ground offensive in the populated areas. The worst-case scenario becomes therefore quite possible, and that would mean thousands and thousands of people killed, not to mention the maimed and wounded, and that is absolutely frightening.

Daniel Finn: If Hamas is going to be seen as a victor even a partial victor coming out of this latest confrontation with Israel, what does it have to do? Is it enough for Hamas to survive? Do they just have to keep standing?

Gilbert Achcar: If Hamas manages to come out of this war standing up, that is. Due to the geographical conditions, they have already suffered a certainly higher proportional rate of casualties in their ranks than Hezbollah did in 2006. The day when Israeli bombing started, the very first day, if you remember, it targeted buildings of the Hamas security force, and the death toll was immediately very heavy. But if at the level of leadership and basic structure they manage to come out preserving more or less their existence without giving any major concession or, let's say, no major concession that is not reciprocated like, "We stop firing rockets but we get guarantees that you, Israel, stop shooting at us and stop embargoing us, strangulating us" – if they come out of this war with a deal of this kind, this would mean an Israeli fiasco and this would be seen for them as a political victory in the same way that Hezbollah achieved one in 2006.

But right now, at the time we are speaking, this is purely hypothetical because we cannot predict how things will evolve. What is actually clear is that at the regional level, if not at the world level, this Israeli onslaught has increased tremendously the popularity of Hamas. We cannot take it for granted, however, that the same applies to the Palestinians in Gaza precisely because of this competition between Hamas and Fatah. On this there are mixed reports. Of course, Fatah supporters will say "Hamas have put us in this terrible situation, we are suffering because of them; of course, Israel is the first to blame, but...", this same "but" that we have heard from some Arab regimes. This is what the Egyptian government, which is very obviously in collusion with this Israeli onslaught, expressed from the very start, and that is what we heard here and there from Arab allies of the United States, the same rhetoric we heard in 2006, the same blame that was put on Hezbollah for Israel's onslaught on Lebanon. The final political outcome for Hamas remains to be seen. It is, I think, too early now to make any assessment for what it will be in the long run or even in the medium term. For the time being, as I said, the only certain thing is for Hamas at the regional level an increasing popularity, which is the almost automatic outcome that you get every time Israel singles out an Arab target and starts striking at it. The target becomes automatically popular because of the hatred for Israel and its permanent aggression in the region: any victim of Israel, and especially any force resisting Israel, is sure of achieving popularity in the region.

Daniel Finn: There has been talk over the last week of a certain amount of discontent among a younger generation of Fatah. There have been reports that Marwan Barghouti has sent messages from his prison cell critical of the statements made by Mahmoud Abbas. Do you think that is likely to take on any substantial form with the current leadership of Fatah being undermined; do you think there's any chance of the Fatah leadership changing course?

Gilbert Achcar: Barghouti is in a sense a reserve card for Fatah. Mahmoud Abbas has already burnt his cards to a great degree. He doesn't have any credibility anymore, but appears as a servile man, a secondary pawn in this regional game. He is not popular even within Fatah, so it is clear that Fatah will be in need of another leading figure immediately or very soon, and Barghouti would be an alternative. But since he is in jail, his fate much depends on Israel-and on Washington, to be sure.

Now, to know how Barghouti would behave if ever he was liberated from jail is hard to tell. The main problem is what kind of relation he would have with the US and their number one Palestinian stooge Muhammad Dahlan. Dahlan and Barghouti were in electoral alliance in the January 2006 election. Does it mean that they will maintain a collaboration and form a cohesive dominant team in the post-Abbas Fatah, or will they be in competition? It remains to be seen.

Daniel Finn: As you said the Egyptian regime in particular and to a greater or lesser extent also all of the pro-US Arab regimes, have been seen as complicit with Israel particularly the Mubarak government. If there is further escalation, if Israel behaves, as you described it, like a wounded animal, using more and more brutal methods against the Palestinians living in Gaza, how difficult is it going to prove for the Egyptian government to be able to contain anger among its own people, which already seems to be very substantial.

Gilbert Achcar: Well, they are not only seen as complicit. They are actually complicit with Israel: They were told about the onslaught before it started and this was reported in the press. The day the onslaught started, the Arabic daily published in London, Al-Quds al-Arabi, ran an article by their correspondent in the West Bank explaining that Israeli foreign minister Tzipi Livni, who had been in Cairo the day before, had told the Egyptian authorities that Israel was going to launch an operation against Hamas. General Suleiman, the head of Egyptian intelligence, asked her that Israel targets specifically Hamas fighters and takes care to spare civilians. Well on the same day the article came out the onslaught started, and it started by targeting police barracks in Gaza. So, on the face of it, it was an onslaught sparing civilians and specifically targeting armed forces. This proves beyond a shadow of a doubt that they were told that this would happen and they did not even tell Hamas, which was taken by surprise when the onslaught started, hence the initial heavy death toll in the ranks of its armed forces.

The Egyptian government and other pro-US Arab regimes wish very much for a weakened Hamas. They are not for wiping out Hamas, as they know that it would entail a huge and traumatizing human cost, if it were possible at all. They would like a weakened Hamas that would have no choice then but to sever its links with Iran and be obliged to depend on them for its survival: This is what they wish. They want a tamed Hamas and therefore look for Israel to do the taming. So, Israel has to teach Hamas a lesson and then Egypt and, behind Egypt, the Saudis and the Jordanians will say to Hamas: "Look, you have no other choice but to cooperate with us; either you join the game under our conditions and sever all links with Iran and Syria, or you will have to face Israel alone and the possibility that it crushes you".

Now if the Israeli operation backfires, they will turn coats immediately, of course, by pure opportunism. They will turn coats and start bashing Israel and multiply statements of condemnation, which don't go very far. The Egyptian regime could upgrade its disagreement with Israel on the issue of international troops on the Egyptian side of the border with Gaza, which Cairo is rejecting and Israel is demanding. There are issues of this kind which could be blown out of proportion, allowing Cairo and fellow Arab regimes to pretend that they do confront Israel, but in a responsible way because they know Israeli military strength and care for the welfare of the people and therefore, they are not like those crazy guys of Hamas, etc. This is their kind of hypocritical discourse.

Daniel Finn: Hezbollah organized some very substantial rallies in Lebanon in solidarity with Hamas and in solidarity with the people of Gaza. Is their support likely to remain political or is there any prospect, as some people have speculated in rather alarmist terms, that Hezbollah might open a second front against Israel on the Northern border.

Gilbert Achcar: I don't think there is any prospect of this kind. It seems that the 3 rockets fired from Lebanon into Northern Israel yesterday were launched by one of the small Palestinian groups linked to Damascus. Hezbollah immediately denied any responsibility and the Lebanese coalition government where Hezbollah is represented condemned unanimously the firing of these rockets. The reality, at this stage, is that you have huge demonstrations and manifestations of political solidarity, but Hezbollah have also drawn the lesson from 2006. If you remember after the 33-Day War in 2006, the Secretary General of Hezbollah, Hassan Nasrallah, said in an interview that had he known that Israel would react the way it reacted to the abduction of its two soldiers on the 12th of July, Hezbollah wouldn't have done it. He was meaning: "Had I known that they would destroy my country and kill 1,500 of my people, I wouldn't have given them a pretext for that". This is what he meant, addressing human feelings.

At the same time, we know that for Israel the abduction was but a pretext: had no soldiers been abducted Israel would have found – or created – whatever pretext in order to do what they tried to do at that time. Hezbollah accepted UN Security Council Resolution 1701, which meant deployment not only of Lebanese troops to Southern Lebanon but also international forces, the UNIFIL, although this is not exactly in the interest of Hezbollah since these forces are heavily composed of NATO forces and are therefore a potential threat to Hezbollah itself. They had to accept them nevertheless because the alternative was to carry on with that horrible war and there were human limits on that level. Hezbollah cannot therefore take what would appear to be a completely irresponsible initiative in opening a second front – especially if it gets no green light for that from both Damascus and Tehran.

On the other hand, how can one expect the Lebanese to open a second front, when the Palestinians on the West Bank themselves, including Hamas, are not opening one: Hamas did not fire rockets from the West Bank. This by the way shows how serious an error was Hamas's decision to seize full power in Gaza alone, thus separating the two Palestinian territories. Not that they should not have pre-empted the coup that Dahlan was busy organizing against them with US and Israeli backing, but they should not have wiped out all Fatah presence in PA institutions as they did. Whereas the strategic need is for the struggle to be built on a pan-regional level, the Palestinian scene itself has been fragmented into two segments. This is a pity.

These events also bring into discussion the whole issue of the strategic choices of weapons. Hamas is resisting heroically, no doubt, but we cannot compare the conditions in Lebanon with the conditions in Palestine. During the years when you had the Israeli occupation of Lebanon, Hezbollah was waging a war of attrition against the occupation, concentrating mainly in Lebanese areas against occupying forces. It even reached with the occupier in April 1996, through US mediation, an agreement which stipulated that: "Armed groups in Lebanon will not carry out attacks by Katyusha rockets or by any kind of weapon into Israel. Israel and those cooperating with it will not fire any kind of weapon at civilians or civilian targets in Lebanon. Beyond this, the two parties commit to ensuring that under no circumstances will civilians be the target of attack and that civilian populated areas and industrial and electrical installations will not be used as launching grounds for attacks". The geographical nature of the Lebanese terrain and the presence of Israeli forces in Lebanese populated areas made a strategy of popular resistance possible, and this triumphed eventually with Israel evacuating Southern Lebanon in what looked like a debacle in 2000.

In the case of Gaza however, Israeli troops had withdrawn from the interior of the Strip and were encircling it. It doesn't make much sense strategically to confront them militarily by launching rockets into populated areas in Southern Israel. The point is that from the point of view of the Palestinian occupied territories, if you drew up a balance-sheet of the Palestinian struggle against the Israeli state since 1967, it is very clear that the peak efficiency of the Palestinian struggle was reached in 1988 with the so-called Revolution of the Stones, the first Intifada, without firearms, suicide bombing, rockets, anything of the kind- just mass mobilization. This is what was most terrible for Israel: it put the Israelis in terrible political difficulty.

There is a lesson to be drawn here. These are matters of strategic understanding which not all forces in the region are sufficiently taking into consideration. There is today a lot of religious-inspired maximalism in the Palestinian struggle, as there was yesterday nationalist-inspired maximalism, but hardly any realistic assessment of the conditions in designing a strategy. Not a strategy of capitulation in the name of "realism", of course, like that of the PLO-I mean the PA, Arafat and now Mahmoud Abbas-but a strategy of resistance and liberation, of popular resistance to impose on Israel whatever strategic goal is feasible in the present condition. And what remains possible in the prevailing objective conditions is to get Israel to withdraw from the 1967 occupied territories, with the possibility for these territories to organize their own government democratically, to enjoy at least political sovereignty – which is not the case presently when you see how Israel and its Western backers reacted to Hamas's electoral victory.

Beyond this immediate goal, the only sensible long-term strategy has to involve a disruption in the Israeli society itself. It cannot be designed as purely from without Israeli society as have been both the PLO's strategy and that of Hamas. There is no possibility to defeat Israel militarily from without: no possibility in conventional terms because its weaponry is much stronger than all surrounding Arab states, not to mention the fact that no part of this environment is willing to confront Israel-not only Egypt and Jordan, but Syria too. A "popular war" for the liberation of the whole of historical Palestine does not make sense, because Israelis are the overwhelming majority in the pre-1967 territory. This is not like an occupying army, whether the US in Vietnam or Afghanistan or Iraq, or Israel in Lebanon. Beyond that, everyone knows that Israel is a nuclear power since the late 1960s. Any thinking built on destroying the

Israeli state from without is therefore irrational, in all senses of the term.

So aside from the requisites of internationalism, i.e., the kind of victory over the Zionist state that is desirable, there is no sensible strategy to defeat it anyway that does not take in account the necessity for a major disruption within Israeli society itself, with a major faction of Israeli society actively opposing the bellicose policies of the Israeli government and fighting for a lasting peaceful settlement based on justice, self-determination and an end to all kinds of discrimination. This is a major, hugely important prerequisite. That is why the Intifada in 1988 was so important: It created a real, deep crisis within Israeli society.

But what we are seeing now is a very high degree of cohesion and unanimity among the Israelis in the most ferocious, severe and brutal aggression of their history and that is something which bodes ill. In such conditions even when you get fiascos like the one in 2006, what do they produce? Not a break of major chunks of the Israeli population away from its government's policy, let alone with Zionism, and their turning anti-war like major portions of the German population in the First World War or the US population during the Vietnam War, but what you get are rather further shifts to the right. That is why the whole picture is very gloomy in the region because, as I said, if this offensive ends in a fiasco, which is what we wish, we know in advance that this means Netanyahu, who is even worse than the present guys. Where all this will end is very difficult to see.

Daniel Finn: It does appear to be a very dangerous time for the Palestinians and perhaps as dangerous a time that it has faced since 1967. There's talk in Israel media circles, in establishment circles, about handing over the Gaza strip to Egyptian authority, handing over populated areas of the West Bank to Jordan. And if that plan or something similar was put into practice, that would surely be fatal for Palestinian national aspirations for many years to come. What steps do you think could be taken by forces within Palestinian society to improve the prospects of the national movement?

Gilbert Achcar: I don't really see things as you described them. First of all, the Jordanian monarchy itself would be rather scared today if it had to resume control of the West Bank. When this was a real prospect, it had already taken into account the rising militancy of the Palestinians, which is why the plans designed by previous King Hussein were federative in nature, that is, plans giving the West Bank, or the West Bank and Gaza, some degree of self-government. But the problem now is that the Jordanian monarchy cannot rely on the likes of Mahmoud Abbas to tame the Palestinian population. They know that they are facing a very radicalized population and that a new junction, a new merge between the Palestinians on the West Bank and Palestinians in Jordan, where they already constitute a majority of the population, would be very dangerous for the Jordanian monarchy. That's the problem.

A renewed merge of the West bank with Jordan would definitely be in the interest of the Palestinians because the so-called independent state in the West Bank and Gaza does not make sense. This is where I fully agree with those who criticize the two-state solution: A so-called independent state does not make sense in the West Bank, if it is to be held hostage between Israel and Jordan as vice and hammer. Therefore, the Palestinian people need the necessary breathing space and outlet provided by Jordan, not to mention the human and familial continuities between the two banks of the River Jordan. There is a natural historical unity of human community between the two banks and for that community to be able to exert self-determination you need a different kind of government in Jordan, a really democratic one and not one where the majority of the population are oppressed by a regime that stirs up ethnical divisions of a tribal nature, as is the case right now.

This is why I don't think that the prospect of a renewed merging of the two banks is one that the Jordanian government is enthusiastic for, or even actively considering. In 1988 King Hussein officially severed the links between his kingdom and the West Bank: Why did he do so? Very simply because in 1988 you had the Intifada in full swing and he understood that the kind of West Bank that the monarchy ruled over since the deal that his father cut with the Zionists in 1948 – the West Bank that his monarchy was able to rule more or less without major trouble until 1967 and that came under Israeli occupation afterwards – had become unmanageable in light of the Intifada. It became a hot potato: too dangerous to handle, and that is why he severed the links officially and abandoned any claims for the West Bank.

Daniel Finn: Do you think the Palestinian political stage is likely to remain the property of Hamas and Fatah for the foreseeable future, or do you think that some of the marginal forces at present have any chance of establishing themselves to a greater extent?

Gilbert Achcar: Well, I don't really see any such prospect presently. I mean, there are no real challengers for the time being to the two major actors, which are Fatah and Hamas. Other existing forces, especially the Palestinian left, lost credibility throughout the years, after having lost so many opportunities. So, one cannot expect a sudden miraculous development, unless some new force arises, which we haven't heard of yet and which would take some time to mature anyway. What you will have under the present conditions are further evolutions from within the two polar forces in Palestinian society – a struggle between different factions within Fatah, and the same for Hamas. Neither of these two forces, because they are big forces and have mass constituencies and memberships, is monolithic. Changes from within them are presently more likely than any unexpected rise of new forces from without.

Now that being said, I wish very strongly that a third force could rise, one which would be a progressive movement based on the left-wing tradition that exists among the Palestinians and that is far from being negligible, even in Gaza, although it is not strong enough to be a counterweight to Fatah or Hamas. I wish very much that some Palestinian left-wing force could emerge as a real major player on the scene. But to be frank, for the time being, aside from hope or wish, this is not a realistic prospect, we don't see any premise for that.

Notes

1. *Haaretz*, 10 /02/2023, https://www.haaretz.com/ israel-news/2023-02-10/ty-article- magazine/.highlight/israels-government-has-neo-nazi- ministers-it-really-does-recall-germany-in-1933/ 00000186-3a49-d80f-abff-7ac9c7ff0000

2. Wikipedia, https://en.wikipedia.org/wiki/ Warsaw_Ghetto_Uprising

3. https://gilbert-achcar.net/narcissistic-compassion

4. *Times of Israel*, 9/10/2023, https://www.timesofis- rael.com/liveblog_entry/defense-minister-announces- complete-siege-of-gaza-no-power-food-or-fuel/

5. G. Achcar, *The Clash of Barbarism, The Making of the New World Disorder* (2nd edition, Saqi Books, 2006).

6. https://gilbert-achcar.net/on-hamas-october-offensive

7. *Haaretz*, 10/02/2023, https://www.haaretz.com/israel-news/2023-02-10/ty-article-magazine/.highlight/israels-government-has-neo-nazi-ministers-it-really-does-recall-germany-in-1933/00000186-3a49-d80f-abff-7ac9c7ff0000

8. Wikipedia, https://en.wikipedia.org/wiki/Deir_Yassin_massacre

9. Wikipedia, https://en.wikipedia.org/wiki/Israeli_disengagement_from_Gaza

10. *Times of Israel*, 22/09/2023, https://www.timesofisrael.com/liveblog_entry/netanyahu-brandishes-map-of-israel-that-includes-west-bank-and-gaza-at-un-speech/

11. *New York Times*, 25/11/2023, https://www.nytimes.com/2023/11/25/world/middleeast/israel-gaza-death-toll.html

12. *Washington Post*, 13/11/2023, https://www.washingtonpost.com/world/interactive/2023/gaza-rising-death-toll-civilians

13. *New York Times*, 10/01/2009, https://www.nytimes.com/2009/01/11/washington/11iran.html?_r=1

Anti*Capitalist Resistance is an organisation of revolutionary socialists. We believe red-green revolution is necessary to meet the compound crisis of humanity and the planet.

We are internationalists, ecosocialists, and anti-capitalist revolutionaries. We oppose imperialism, nationalism, and militarism, and all forms of discrimination, oppression, and bigotry. We support the self-organisation of women, Black people, disabled people, and LGBTQI+ people. We support all oppressed people fighting imperialism and forms of apartheid, and struggling for self-determination, including the people of Palestine.

We favour mass resistance to neoliberal capitalism. We work inside existing mass organisations, but we believe grassroots struggle to be the core of effective resistance, and that the emancipation of the working class and the oppressed will be the act of the working class and the oppressed ourselves.

We reject forms of left organisation that focus exclusively on electoralism and social-democratic reforms. We also oppose top-down 'democratic centralist' models. We favour a pluralist organisation that can learn from struggles at home and across the world.

We aim to build a united organisation, rooted in the struggles of the working class and the oppressed, and committed to debate, initiative, and self-activity. We are for social transformation, based on mass participatory democracy.

info@anticapitalistresistance.org
www.anticapitalistresistance.org

ABOUT RESISTANCE BOOKS

Resistance Books is a radical publisher of internationalist, ecosocialist, and feminist books. Resistance Books publishes books in collaboration with Anti*Capitalist Resistance (anticapitalistresistance.org), the International Institute for Research and Education (iire.org), and the Fourth International (fourth.international). For further information, including a full list of titles available and how to order them, go to the Resistance Books website.

info@resistancebooks.org
www.resistancebooks.org

Making Sense of Russia's Invasion of Ukraine
Paul Le Blanc

Capitalist China and Socialist Revolution
Simon Hannah

Ecosocialism Not Extinction
Allan Todd

Stalinist Realism and Open Communism: Malignant Mirror or Free Association
Ian Parker

Radical Psychoanalysis and Anti-capitalist Action
Ian Parker

Mind Fuck: The Mass Psychology of Creeping Fascism
Neil Faulkner

Alienation, Spectacle, and Revolution: A critical Marxist essay
Neil Faulkner

Why We Need Anti-capitalist Resistance
Simon Hannah

All titles in the pocket book series are £5 from www.resistancebooks.org.

E-books of these titles are available from online retailers.

Milton Keynes UK
Ingram Content Group UK Ltd.
UKHW022222071223
433949UK00014B/288

9 781872 242194